The Fraction Book

Fractions, Decimals and Percentages

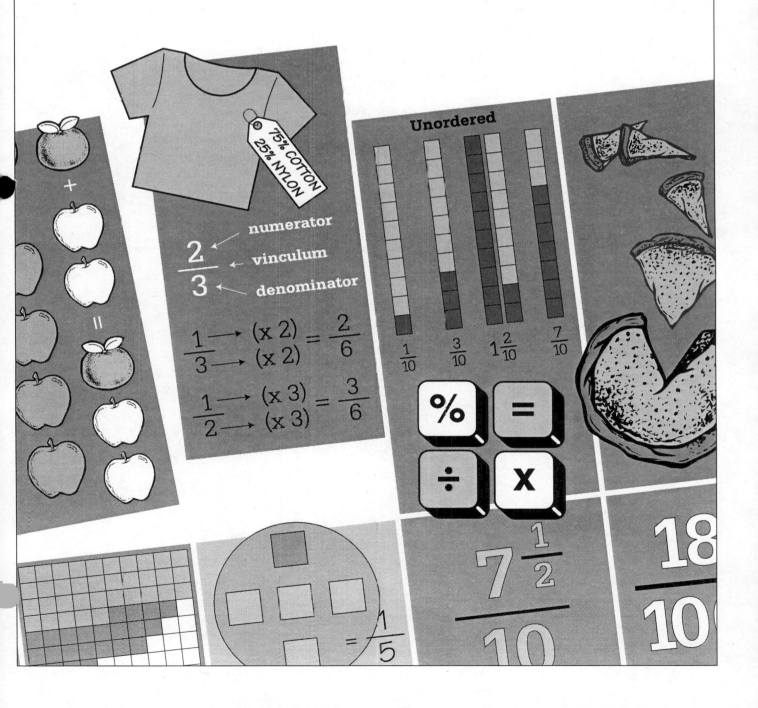

Order Number 2-5029
ISBN 978-1-885111-42-5

P Q R S T 13 12 11 10 09

395 Main Street
Rowley, MA 01969
www.didax.com

Introduction

Fractions, Decimals and Percentages all deal with 'a part of' something, whether it be 'part of a whole' or 'part of a group'. This area of mathematics has often caused problems for both teachers and students alike; this concern however, is unnecessary if the correct grounding is given and basic concepts are understood.

This blackline master provides an introduction to fractions, decimals and percentages. The activities provide a framework for the students to develop confidence and understanding in this often misunderstood area of mathematics.

Review pages are provided and should be used to assess the progress of the students.

The Early Fraction Book is the title that precedes this book and provides a developmental study of fractions from their simplest form to more difficult uses.

Table of Contents

Teacher Information

Introduction

Fractions, decimals and percentages all deal with 'a part of' something, whether it be 'part of a whole' or 'part of a group'. This area of mathematics has often caused problems for both teachers and students alike; this concern however, is unnecessary if the correct grounding is given and basic concepts are understood.

This blackline master provides an introduction to fractions, decimals, and percentages. The activities provide a framework for the teacher and student to develop confidence and understanding in this often misunderstood area of mathematics.

It is vital that repeated practical activities are provided so that a solid understanding of basic concepts is developed. Activities in this book should be repeated using concrete materials and a variety of different objects. Fractions, like all areas of mathematics, are an enjoyable subject properly when understood.

A language component has been provided through the inclusion of several pages of text and comprehension questions. This serves two main purposes:

(i) to link mathematics directly to language; and

(ii) to provide students with a written description of what they are learning.

Review pages are provided and should be used to assess the progress of students.

Teaching Strategies

Fractions, decimals and percentages are areas of mathematics that have common links. Each is a mathematical method of representing a portion or 'part of' some thing or group of things. Each has many and varied uses which children and adults have regular contact with.

It is vital that teaching strategies used when introducing these concepts are based on practical activities. The activities in this book provide an introduction and framework for further practical application. Wherever possible, links should be made to situations and events that students can directly relate to. The use of manipulatives is very important to ensure a solid understanding.

Fractions: use commercially produced manipulatives, as well as readily available materials including food, groups of objects (including the class) and situations where a fraction of a single item, or group of items can be represented.

Decimals: the money system is the best method of introducing decimals and then this can be developed further by using manipulatives such as multi-based blocks.

Percentage: the usage of percentage needs to be related to practical situations and can also be linked closely with fractions and decimals. The calculation of test scores, sporting statistics and similar situations are good practical examples.

WISH I WAS HALF OF A HUNDRED AGAIN!

The following is a lesson development using one of the pages in this book. It is an example of how the activity could be introduced, developed and extended.

Activity   Parts of a whole: page 7

Introductory Work

To be at this stage, students should have a basic understanding of fractions. If not, they should use the book *The Early Fraction Book* before working at this level. The purpose of this activity is to review and consolidate the concept that a fraction is a number that represents a part of a whole.

Discussion should center on where, when and how we use fractions in our daily lives. Ask students to make a list independently and then compare with their group/class. Compare how some fractions are a part of unit such as a fraction of a piece of chocolate, and others are a part of a group of objects such as a group of children. This lesson focuses on the former.

Completing the Worksheet

The following is a suggestion for the development and extension of this activity.

The completion of this activity will provide the teacher with information regarding the student's level of knowledge in this area. This activity can be supplemented by using fraction cakes and multi-based blocks.

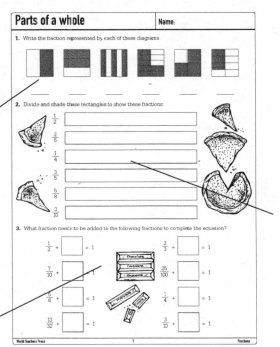

The intention of this activity is to consolidate the understanding that fractions are **equal** parts. The rectangles should be divided equally to demonstrate this understanding.

Practical activities using fraction cakes can precede and follow this activity. The understanding to emphasize is that fractions are a part of a whole.

Extension

Extension of this activity should be based on consolidating the concepts introduced. This should be done using manipulatives and experiences that students can relate to. In addition, students can proceed to reviewing that fractions are also parts of groups of objects.

Fractions

Name:

The dictionary tells us that fractions are: *a part of a whole number; a small part, piece, or amount.*

You have learned that in mathematics fractions are:

1. equal parts of a whole number, e.g. $\frac{1}{2}$ of a chocolate bar, or;

2. equal parts of a group of objects, e.g. $\frac{1}{2}$ of a bag of marbles.

Before the introduction of the decimal system, children needed to learn a lot more about fractions, as this was the only way to show a part of a whole number. Today, the use of fractions is still very important. We use fractions to represent basic units with denominations to twelve.

In the past, using fractions such as $\frac{13}{32}$ and $\frac{17}{64}$ to describe shares of objects or groups of objects were common. Today these fractions have been replaced by decimals and the calculations are often done with calculators or computers.

Writing fractions is done differently than whole numbers. A fraction is made up of a numerator and a denominator. If the numerator is smaller than the denominator the fraction is called

$$\frac{2}{3}$$

numerator – tells us how many parts of the whole there are.

denominator – tells us how many parts are in the whole.

a **proper fraction**. If the numerator is larger than the denominator the fraction is called an **improper fraction**. If a fraction is accompanied by a whole number it is called a **mixed number**.

1. On the back of this sheet, explain, by using diagrams, how a fraction can be part of a whole number as well as part of a group of objects.

2. Why was the learning of fractions more complicated 50 years ago?

   _____

   _____

3. Why are difficult calculations easier to do in today's classrooms?

   _____

4. List three uses for fractions in today's society.

   _____

   _____

5. Describe the three parts of a written fraction. .

   _____

   _____

   _____

Parts of a whole

1. Write the fraction represented by each of these diagrams.

_____   _____   _____   _____   _____   _____

2. Divide and shade these rectangles to show these fractions.

$\frac{1}{2}$

$\frac{2}{5}$

$\frac{1}{4}$

$\frac{3}{5}$

$\frac{5}{8}$

$\frac{3}{10}$

3. What fraction needs to be added to the following fractions to complete the equation?

$\frac{1}{2}$ + ⬜ = 1 $\frac{2}{3}$ + ⬜ = 1

$\frac{7}{10}$ + ⬜ = 1 $\frac{25}{100}$ + ⬜ = 1

$\frac{5}{8}$ + ⬜ = 1 $\frac{1}{4}$ + ⬜ = 1

$\frac{13}{32}$ + ⬜ = 1 $\frac{3}{10}$ + ⬜ = 1

Parts of a set

1. Write the fraction that matches these diagrams.

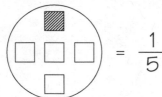 = $\dfrac{1}{5}$ 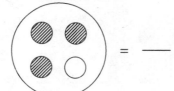 = ———   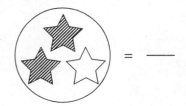 = ———

 = ———    = ———   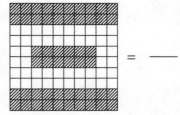 = ———

2. Draw and color a set of objects that represents each of these fractions.

$\dfrac{3}{4}$

$\dfrac{2}{5}$

$\dfrac{11}{12}$

$\dfrac{5}{8}$

3. Write the fraction and the decimal that describe these diagrams.

 = ——— = O._____    = ——— = O._____

 = ——— = O._____   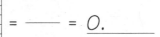 = ——— = O._____

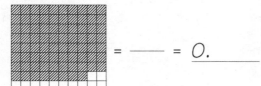 = ——— = O._____   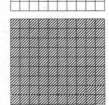 = ——— = O._____

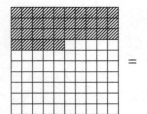
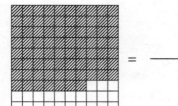
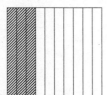
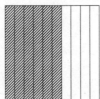

Kinds of fractions (1)

$\dfrac{1}{2}$ is a **proper fraction**, because its denominator is larger than its numerator.

$1\dfrac{1}{2}$ is a **mixed number**, because it is a mix of a whole number and a fraction.

$\dfrac{3}{2}$ is the same number, written as an **improper fraction**.
The numerator is larger than the denominator.

To change an improper fraction to a mixed number you take out the whole numbers to leave a simple fraction.

$$\dfrac{7}{5} = \dfrac{5}{5} + \dfrac{2}{5}$$

$$\dfrac{7}{5} = 1 + \dfrac{2}{5}$$

To change a mixed number to an improper fraction you convert the whole number to fraction form.

$$1\dfrac{3}{4} = \dfrac{4}{4} + \dfrac{3}{4}$$

$$= \dfrac{7}{4}$$

Change these improper fractions to mixed numbers by coloring the diagrams.

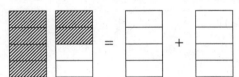

$$\dfrac{6}{4} = \underline{} + \underline{}$$

$$= \underline{}$$

$$\dfrac{5}{2} = \underline{} + \underline{} + \underline{}$$

$$= \underline{}$$

Change these mixed numbers to improper fractions by coloring the diagrams.

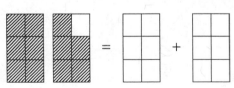
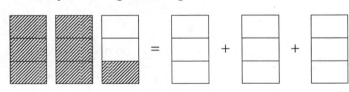

$$1\dfrac{5}{6} = \underline{} + \underline{}$$

$$= \underline{}$$

$$2\dfrac{1}{3} = \underline{} + \underline{} + \underline{}$$

$$= \underline{}$$

Kinds of fractions (2)

Name:

Change these improper fractions to mixed numbers.

$\dfrac{7}{5}$ = —— + ——

= ——

$\dfrac{7}{3}$ = —— + —— + ——

= ——

$\dfrac{6}{2}$ = —— + —— + ——

= ——

$\dfrac{27}{10}$ = —— + —— + ——

= ——

$\dfrac{137}{100}$ = —— + ——

= ——

$\dfrac{250}{100}$ = —— + —— + ——

= ——

$\dfrac{13}{7}$ = —— + ——

= ——

$\dfrac{32}{16}$ = —— + ——

= ——

$\dfrac{22}{5}$ = — + — + — + — + —

= ——

$\dfrac{20}{8}$ =

=

$\dfrac{14}{12}$ =

=

$\dfrac{21}{9}$ =

=

Change these mixed numbers to improper fractions.

$1\dfrac{1}{3}$ = —— + ——

= ——

$1\dfrac{7}{10}$ = —— + ——

= ——

$2\dfrac{3}{4}$ = —— + —— + ——

= ——

$1\dfrac{15}{100}$ = —— + ——

= ——

$2\dfrac{75}{100}$ = —— + —— + ——

= ——

$3\dfrac{1}{4}$ = — + — + — + ——

= ——

$1\dfrac{3}{7}$ = —— + ——

= ——

$2\dfrac{1}{16}$ = —— + —— + ——

= ——

$3\dfrac{7}{20}$ = — + — + — + ——

= ——

$1\dfrac{37}{50}$ =

=

$2\dfrac{7}{9}$ =

=

$1\dfrac{2}{3}$ =

=

Equivalent fractions (1)

Name:

Equivalent means '*equal in value*'. Fractions can look different but be equivalent.

For example:

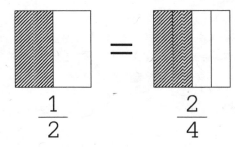

$$\frac{1}{2} = \frac{2}{4}$$

To make equivalent fractions follow this rule:

Multiply the fraction by one, in the form of a whole fraction, e.g. $\frac{4}{4}$.

Look at the following equivalent fractions and how they were made.

$$\frac{1 \longrightarrow}{2 \longrightarrow} \frac{\mathbf{x\,2}}{\mathbf{x\,2}} = \frac{2}{4} \qquad\qquad \frac{2 \longrightarrow}{3 \longrightarrow} \frac{\mathbf{x\,3}}{\mathbf{x\,3}} = \frac{6}{9}$$

$$\frac{1 \longrightarrow}{4 \longrightarrow} \frac{\mathbf{x\,4}}{\mathbf{x\,4}} = \frac{4}{16} \qquad\qquad \frac{3 \longrightarrow}{5 \longrightarrow} \frac{\mathbf{x\,6}}{\mathbf{x\,6}} = \frac{18}{30}$$

To make more equivalent fractions for these examples, you can multiply the fraction by a different **whole fraction**. For example, if you multiply $\frac{1}{2}$ by the whole fractions $\frac{2}{2}$, $\frac{3}{3}$, $\frac{4}{4}$, etc. you get the equivalent fractions $\frac{2}{4}$, $\frac{3}{6}$, $\frac{4}{8}$, etc.

---

1. Write 5 equivalent fractions for $\frac{1}{3}$ in the space provided below.

   ____ ____ ____ ____ ____

2. Write 5 equivalent fractions for $\frac{3}{4}$ in the space provided below.

   ____ ____ ____ ____ ____

3. Write 5 equivalent fractions for $\frac{2}{5}$ in the space provided below.

   ____ ____ ____ ____ ____

Equivalent fractions (2)

Name:

Write two equivalent fractions for each of these fractions.

1. $\dfrac{2}{3}$ = _____ = _____

2. $\dfrac{7}{10}$ = _____ = _____

3. $\dfrac{15}{100}$ = _____ = _____

4. $\dfrac{3}{5}$ = _____ = _____

5. $\dfrac{3}{8}$ = _____ = _____

6. $\dfrac{4}{8}$ = _____ = _____

7. $\dfrac{2}{5}$ = _____ = _____

8. $\dfrac{1}{9}$ = _____ = _____

9. $\dfrac{3}{4}$ = _____ = _____

10. $\dfrac{9}{10}$ = _____ = _____

Which is the simplest way of writing one-half out of these equivalent fractions?

$$\dfrac{1}{2} \quad \dfrac{2}{4} \quad \dfrac{3}{6} \quad \dfrac{4}{8}$$

The answer is of course $\dfrac{1}{2}$. This is the way to show one-half as a fraction.

To simplify a fraction we find a number which will divide into both the numerator and the denominator evenly, leaving no remainder.

For example, to simplify the fraction $\dfrac{6}{10}$, we divide the numerator and the denominator by 2:

$$\dfrac{6}{10} \begin{array}{c} \longrightarrow \div 2 \\ \longrightarrow \div 2 \end{array} = \dfrac{3}{5}$$

So $\dfrac{3}{5}$ is the simplified fraction for $\dfrac{6}{10}$.

Simplify these fractions by dividing the numerator and the denominator by the same number.

1. $\dfrac{15}{20}$ = _____ (divide both by ☐)

2. $\dfrac{2}{10}$ = _____ (divide both by ☐)

3. $\dfrac{15}{18}$ = _____ (divide both by ☐)

4. $\dfrac{5}{10}$ = _____ (divide both by ☐)

Common denominator (1)

Name:

To add and subtract fractions each fraction must have a **common denominator** – they must be the same thing. This is just like adding objects. For example,

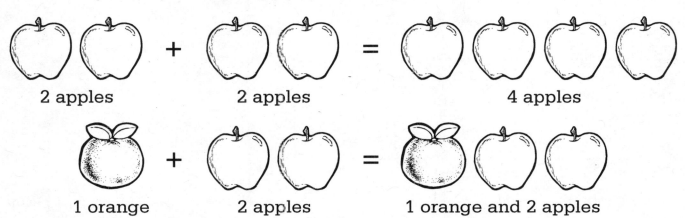

2 apples   +   2 apples   =   4 apples

1 orange   +   2 apples   =   1 orange and 2 apples

We can get an easy answer for the first equation but the second answer is the same as the fraction problem. To get an answer for the second equation we must find something that the orange and apples have in common.

So what do apples and oranges have in common? Apples and oranges are both **fruit**!
We can now reword the problem to read:

1 piece   +   2 pieces   =   3 pieces
of fruit   of fruit   of fruit

We have found a common element or factor.

Find the common element in these problems:

1. 1 station wagon + 2 hatchbacks   = _____

2. 3 boys + 3 girls   = _____

3. 2 daisies + 5 daffodils   = _____

4. 1 teddy bear + 1 action figure + 1 toy car   = _____

Write two problems of your own:

5. _____   = _____

6. _____   = _____

Common denominator (2)

To find **common denominators** in fractions we must find a number that all the denominators will divide evenly into.

For example, look at the fractions $\frac{1}{2}$ and $\frac{1}{3}$.

The denominators for these fractions are 2 and 3. A number that 2 **and** 3 will divide into evenly is 6. We can express both of these fractions as sixths, and so give them both a common denominator. This is how it is done:

$$\frac{1}{2} \longrightarrow \frac{\text{x } 3}{\text{x } 3} = \frac{3}{6}$$

To change the denominator in $\frac{1}{2}$ from 2 to 6 we multiply the fraction by $\frac{3}{3}$.

$$\frac{1}{3} \longrightarrow \frac{\text{x } 2}{\text{x } 2} = \frac{2}{6}$$

To change the denominator in $\frac{1}{3}$ from 3 to 6 we multiply the fraction by $\frac{2}{2}$.

Once we express $\frac{1}{2}$ and $\frac{1}{3}$ as fractions with common denominators, we can add them:

$$\frac{1}{2} \quad + \quad \frac{1}{3} \quad = \quad \frac{3}{6} \quad + \quad \frac{2}{6}$$

$$= \quad \frac{5}{6}$$

Find a common denominator for these fraction pairs.

1. $\frac{1}{2}$, $\frac{1}{4}$ Lowest common denominator = ☐

2. $\frac{1}{2}$, $\frac{1}{5}$ Lowest common denominator = ☐

3. $\frac{1}{3}$, $\frac{1}{8}$ Lowest common denominator = ☐

4. $\frac{1}{3}$, $\frac{1}{6}$ Lowest common denominator = ☐

5. $\frac{1}{4}$, $\frac{1}{6}$ Lowest common denominator = ☐

6. $\frac{1}{5}$, $\frac{1}{10}$ Lowest common denominator = ☐

7. $\frac{1}{2}$, $\frac{1}{8}$ Lowest common denominator = ☐

8. $\frac{1}{3}$, $\frac{1}{4}$ Lowest common denominator = ☐

9. $\frac{1}{9}$, $\frac{1}{5}$ Lowest common denominator = ☐

10. $\frac{1}{9}$, $\frac{1}{4}$ Lowest common denominator = ☐

Common denominator (3)

Many fraction pairs have more than one common denominator.

For example, for the fraction pair of $\frac{1}{2}$ and $\frac{1}{4}$, the common denominators are 4, 8, 12, 16, 20, etc.

In this case, 4 is known as the **lowest common denominator**. That is, it is the lowest number which is divisible by the denominators 2 and 4, without leaving a remainder:

For the fraction $\frac{1}{4}$, 4 ÷ 2 = 2 with no remainder.

For the fraction $\frac{1}{2}$, 2 ÷ 2 = 1 with no remainder.

Find the lowest common denominator for the fraction pairs below, and two other common denominators as well.

1. $\frac{1}{2}, \frac{1}{4}$ Lowest common denominator = ☐   Other common denominators = ☐ , ☐

2. $\frac{1}{5}, \frac{1}{10}$ Lowest common denominator = ☐   Other common denominators = ☐ , ☐

3. $\frac{1}{2}, \frac{1}{5}$ Lowest common denominator = ☐   Other common denominators = ☐ , ☐

4. $\frac{1}{2}, \frac{1}{8}$ Lowest common denominator = ☐   Other common denominators = ☐ , ☐

5. $\frac{1}{10}, \frac{1}{20}$ Lowest common denominator = ☐   Other common denominators = ☐ , ☐

Find the lowest common denominator for these fraction pairs.

1. $\frac{1}{3}, \frac{1}{7}$ Lowest common denominator = ☐   7. $\frac{1}{5}, \frac{1}{10}$ Lowest common denominator = ☐

2. $\frac{1}{2}, \frac{1}{10}$ Lowest common denominator = ☐   8. $\frac{1}{2}, \frac{1}{8}$ Lowest common denominator = ☐

3. $\frac{1}{6}, \frac{1}{9}$ Lowest common denominator = ☐   9. $\frac{1}{3}, \frac{1}{4}$ Lowest common denominator = ☐

4. $\frac{1}{4}, \frac{1}{5}$ Lowest common denominator = ☐   10. $\frac{1}{9}, \frac{1}{5}$ Lowest common denominator = ☐

5. $\frac{1}{25}, \frac{25}{100}$ Lowest common denominator = ☐   11. $\frac{1}{8}, \frac{1}{9}$ Lowest common denominator = ☐

6. $\frac{1}{2}, \frac{1}{9}$ Lowest common denominator = ☐   12. $\frac{2}{5}, \frac{21}{25}$ Lowest common denominator = ☐

Common denominator (4)

When you have found a **common denominator** for a fraction pair, you can add them together.

For example, take the fraction pair $\frac{1}{3}$ and $\frac{1}{4}$.

The common denominator for these two fractions is 12.

Therefore, $\frac{1}{3} + \frac{1}{4} = \frac{4}{12} + \frac{3}{12}$

$$= \frac{7}{12}$$

Find the lowest common denominator for these fraction pairs and then use it to add the fractions.

1. $\frac{1}{4}, \frac{1}{5}$ Lowest common denominator = ☐   ——— + ——— = ——— + ———

= ———

2. $\frac{2}{3}, \frac{1}{4}$ Lowest common denominator = ☐   ——— + ——— = ——— + ———

= ———

3. $\frac{2}{5}, \frac{1}{2}$ Lowest common denominator = ☐   ——— + ——— = ——— + ———

= ———

4. $\frac{17}{25}, \frac{1}{5}$ Lowest common denominator = ☐   ——— + ——— = ——— + ———

= ———

This is Harder!

Find the common denominator for these groups of fractions and add them on the back of this sheet.

1. $\frac{1}{2}, \frac{1}{4}, \frac{1}{3}$ Common denominator = ☐

4. $\frac{1}{4}, \frac{3}{8}, \frac{1}{2}$ Common denominator = ☐

2. $\frac{1}{5}, \frac{1}{10}, \frac{1}{3}$ Common denominator = ☐

5. $\frac{1}{3}, \frac{1}{6}, \frac{1}{9}$ Common denominator = ☐

3. $\frac{1}{2}, \frac{1}{10}, \frac{1}{20}$ Common denominator = ☐

6. $\frac{2}{5}, \frac{21}{25}, \frac{1}{20}$ Common denominator = ☐

Converting to hundredths (1)

Name:

A way to express fractions as decimals is to convert them to hundredths. Complete the diagrams below to convert the fraction on the left into a decimal number (out of 100).

1.

$\dfrac{1}{2}$ = 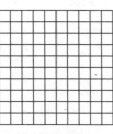 = [grid] = $\dfrac{}{100}$ = **0.** [ ]

2.

$\dfrac{1}{4}$ = 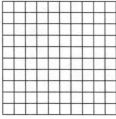 = [grid] = $\dfrac{}{100}$ = **0.** [ ]

3.

$\dfrac{1}{5}$ = 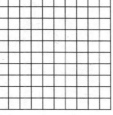 = [grid] = $\dfrac{}{100}$ = **0.** [ ]

4.

$\dfrac{1}{10}$ = 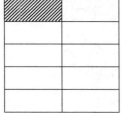 = [grid] = $\dfrac{}{100}$ = **0.** [ ]

Write these fractions as hundredths and decimals.

1. $\dfrac{2}{4}$ = $\dfrac{}{100}$ = **0.** [ ]

2. $\dfrac{7}{10}$ = $\dfrac{}{100}$ = **0.** [ ]

3. $\dfrac{2}{10}$ = $\dfrac{}{100}$ = **0.** [ ]

4. $\dfrac{3}{10}$ = $\dfrac{}{100}$ = **0.** [ ]

5. $\dfrac{4}{5}$ = $\dfrac{}{100}$ = **0.** [ ]

6. $\dfrac{2}{5}$ = $\dfrac{}{100}$ = **0.** [ ]

7. $\dfrac{6}{10}$ = $\dfrac{}{100}$ = **0.** [ ]

8. $\dfrac{3}{4}$ = $\dfrac{}{100}$ = **0.** [ ]

Converting to hundredths (2)

Name:

To convert a fraction to hundredths we follow the same rule as equivalent fractions.
We multiply the fraction by the whole fraction which gives a denominator of 100.

For example, to convert the fraction $\frac{1}{2}$

to a fraction out of 100 we multiply it by the whole fraction $\frac{50}{50}$:

$$\frac{1}{2} \times \frac{50}{50} = \frac{50}{100}$$

whole fraction

WISH I WAS HALF OF A HUNDRED AGAIN!

Therefore, $\frac{1}{2}$ becomes $\frac{50}{100}$, which is 0.5 as a decimal.

Convert these fractions into decimals.

1. $\frac{1}{10}$ = $\frac{}{100}$ = $\boxed{0.}$

2. $\frac{1}{5}$ = $\frac{}{100}$ = $\boxed{0.}$

3. $\frac{1}{20}$ = $\frac{}{100}$ = $\boxed{0.}$

4. $\frac{15}{20}$ = $\frac{}{100}$ = $\boxed{0.}$

5. $\frac{6}{20}$ = $\frac{}{100}$ = $\boxed{0.}$

6. $\frac{1}{25}$ = $\frac{}{100}$ = $\boxed{0.}$

7. $\frac{17}{25}$ = $\frac{}{100}$ = $\boxed{0.}$

8. $\frac{8}{10}$ = $\frac{}{100}$ = $\boxed{0.}$

Convert these decimals back into fractions. Simplify the fractions wherever possible.

1. 0.95 = $\frac{}{100}$ = $\frac{}{}$

2. 0.6 = $\frac{}{100}$ = $\frac{}{}$

3. 0.75 = $\frac{}{100}$ = $\frac{}{}$

4. 0.33 = $\frac{}{100}$ = $\frac{}{}$

5. 0.9 = $\frac{}{100}$ = $\frac{}{}$

6. 0.2 = $\frac{}{100}$ = $\frac{}{}$

7. 0.02 = $\frac{}{100}$ = $\frac{}{}$

8. 0.85 = $\frac{}{100}$ = $\frac{}{}$

Ordering fractions (1)

Name:

Look at the example below to see how fractions are ordered from smallest to largest.

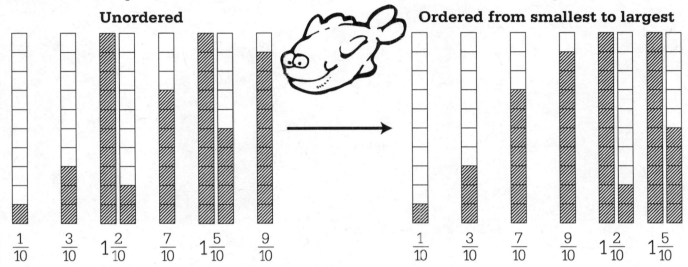

Unordered

$\frac{1}{10}$ $\frac{3}{10}$ $1\frac{2}{10}$ $\frac{7}{10}$ $1\frac{5}{10}$ $\frac{9}{10}$

Ordered from smallest to largest

$\frac{1}{10}$ $\frac{3}{10}$ $\frac{7}{10}$ $\frac{9}{10}$ $1\frac{2}{10}$ $1\frac{5}{10}$

Color these fractions on the diagram and then order them from smallest to largest:

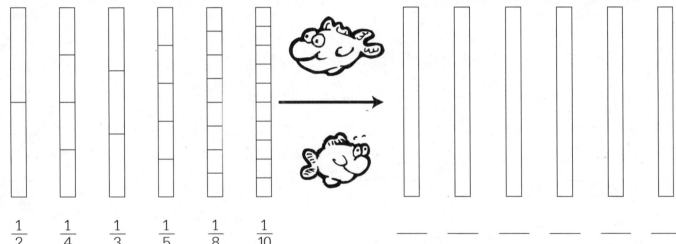

Unordered

$\frac{1}{2}$ $\frac{1}{4}$ $\frac{1}{3}$ $\frac{1}{5}$ $\frac{1}{8}$ $\frac{1}{10}$

Ordered from smallest to largest

____ ____ ____ ____ ____ ____

Place these fractions in ascending order (from smallest to largest), by first expressing them with a common denominator.

		common denominator			**in ascending order**	
1. $\frac{1}{3}$, $\frac{2}{5}$, $\frac{1}{2}$	____	____	____	____	____	____
2. $\frac{3}{4}$, $\frac{1}{2}$, $\frac{3}{8}$	____	____	____	____	____	____
3. $\frac{3}{10}$, $\frac{2}{5}$, $\frac{15}{100}$	____	____	____	____	____	____
4. $\frac{3}{5}$, $\frac{7}{10}$, $\frac{65}{100}$	____	____	____	____	____	____

Ordering fractions (2)

Simplify these fractions. The first has been done for you.

$$\frac{15}{100}, \frac{60}{100}, \frac{50}{100}, \frac{75}{100}, \frac{25}{100}, \frac{20}{100}$$

$\frac{3}{20}$ _____ _____ _____ _____ _____

Now order the simplified fractions in order from smallest to largest.

_____ _____ _____ _____ _____ _____

Add these fractions together and order the answers.

1. $\frac{1}{5} + \frac{2}{5}$ = _____

  $\frac{1}{2} + \frac{1}{6}$ = _____ + _____ = _____

  $\frac{1}{3} + \frac{1}{4}$ = _____ + _____ = _____

  $\frac{1}{4} + \frac{1}{4}$ = _____

Answers in order from smallest to largest:

_____ _____ _____ _____

2. $\frac{1}{10} + \frac{1}{9}$ = _____ + _____ = _____

  $\frac{2}{10} + \frac{3}{5}$ = _____ + _____ = _____

  $\frac{1}{3} + \frac{2}{3}$ = _____ =

  $\frac{5}{6} + \frac{1}{12}$ = _____ + _____ = _____

Answers in order from smallest to largest:

_____ _____ _____ _____

---

3. $\frac{2}{5} + \frac{1}{6}$ = _____ + _____ = _____

  $\frac{1}{2} + \frac{1}{8}$ = _____ + _____ = _____

  $\frac{3}{8} + \frac{7}{16}$ = _____ + _____ = _____

  $\frac{5}{100} + \frac{25}{100}$ = _____ = _____

Answers in order from smallest to largest:

_____ _____ _____ _____

4. $\frac{1}{5} + \frac{1}{3}$ = _____ + _____ = _____

  $\frac{2}{5} + \frac{1}{4}$ = _____ + _____ = _____

  $\frac{1}{2} + \frac{1}{4}$ = _____ + _____ = _____

  $\frac{3}{4} + \frac{1}{8}$ = _____ + _____ = _____

Answers in order from smallest to largest:

_____ _____ _____ _____

Fractions and decimals

Name: _____

1. Color these fractions and write them as decimals.

$$\frac{12}{100} \qquad\qquad \frac{45}{100} \qquad\qquad \frac{76}{100} \qquad\qquad \frac{34}{100}$$

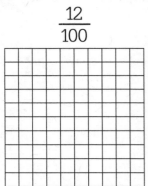

_____   _____   _____   _____

2. Write these fractions as decimals.

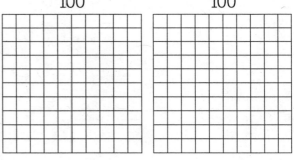

(i) twenty-seven hundredths _____

(ii) nine hundredths _____

(iii) seventy-five hundredths _____

(iv) one hundredth _____

3. Color the grids to match these decimals. (Numbers to the left of the decimal point are whole numbers. Numbers to the right of the decimal point are decimal fractions.)

0.75

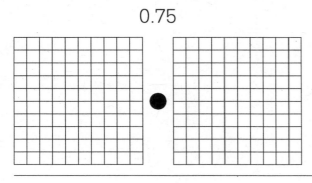

1.27

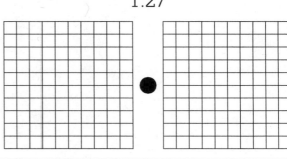

0.03

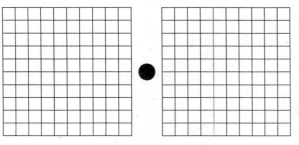

1.85

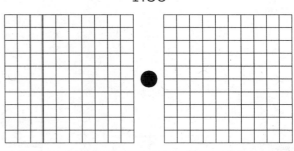

Centimeters and meters

Name: _____

One hundred centimeters equal one meter. Any measurement less than a hundred centimeters is a fraction, or part of, one meter. These measurements can be written in *decimal form*.

1. Write these centimeter measurements as meters in decimal form.
   For example 156 cm = 1 meter and 56 cm = 1.56 m.

   (i)   175 cm _____

   (ii)   105 cm _____

   (iii)   215 cm _____

   (iv)   176 cm _____

   (v)   95 cm _____

   (vi)   345 cm _____

   (vii)   10 cm _____

   (viii)   271 cm _____

2. The following are the measurements taken of students at Milby Primary School.
   Convert the measurements to meters and order them from smallest to largest.

Name	Height in centimeters	Height in meters	Order
John	154 cm		
Mary	165 cm		
Chris	134 cm		
Martin	125 cm		
Andrea	143 cm		
Richard	121 cm		
Michelle	149 cm		
Mark	137 cm		

Tenths and hundredths

Name:

To divide a whole number into tenths we need ten equal parts. This can be done like this:

Each one of these tenths can be written as a fraction and a decimal.

$$\boxed{} = \frac{1}{10} = 0.1$$

Each tenth can be divided again into a further ten equal parts. Each tenth divided into a further ten will give us one hundred parts, or hundredths.

Each one of these hundredths can be written as a fraction and a decimal.

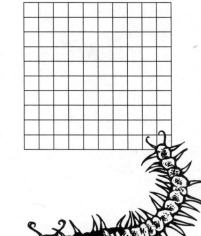

$$\square = \frac{1}{100} = 0.01$$

Write these fractions as decimals.

1. $\dfrac{2}{10} =$ _____

2. $\dfrac{24}{100} =$ _____

3. $\dfrac{9}{10} =$ _____

4. $\dfrac{65}{100} =$ _____

5. $\dfrac{7}{100} =$ _____

6. $\dfrac{5}{10} =$ _____

7. $\dfrac{147}{100} =$ _____

8. $\dfrac{201}{100} =$ _____

9. $\dfrac{7}{10} =$ _____

10. $\dfrac{8}{10} =$ _____

Ordering decimals (1)

Name:

1. Write the following decimals and place in order from smallest to largest.

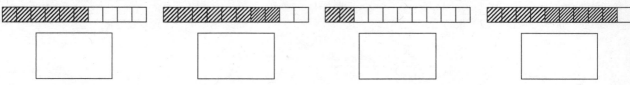

[ ]   [ ]   [ ]   [ ]

_____ , _____ , _____ , _____

2. Write the following decimals and place them in order from smallest to largest.

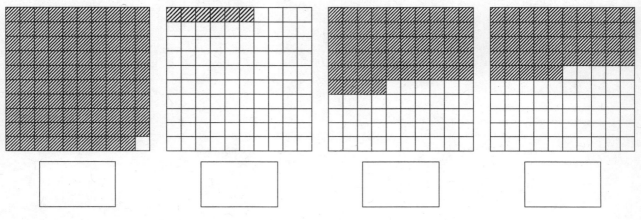

[ ]   [ ]   [ ]   [ ]

_____ , _____ , _____ , _____

3. Place the following decimals in order from smallest to largest.

0.1   0.09   0.21   0.8   0.11

_____ , _____ , _____ , _____ , _____

4. Place the following decimals in order from smallest to largest.

0.61   0.09   0.27   0.55   0.11

_____ , _____ , _____ , _____ , _____

5.   Color 0.4 on this grid.   Color 0.04 on this grid.

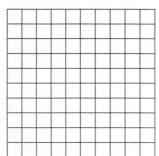  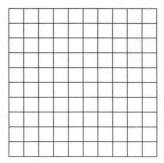

How many times bigger is 0.4 than 0.04? _____

Ordering decimals (2)

Name:

1. Write the following decimals and place in order from smallest to largest.

[ ]   [ ]   [ ]   [ ]

_____ , _____ , _____ , _____

2. Write the following decimals and place them in order from smallest to largest.

[ ]   [ ]   [ ]   [ ]

_____ , _____ , _____ , _____

3. Write the larger number of each pair.

(i) 0.3 and 0.03 _____

(iii) 0.45 and 0.5 _____

(ii) 0.23 and 0.32 _____

(iv) 0.78 and 0.87 _____

4. Which is the larger number, one tenth or one hundredth? _____

5. Write the order for these decimals from smallest to largest.

     0.34   0.4   0.56   0.75   0.57   0.43   0.04   0.3

_____ , _____ , _____ , _____ ,

_____ , _____ , _____ , _____ .

6. Measure the height in meters of five of your friends and order them in size.
Record your answers in decimal form in the space provided below.

Friend					
Height (m)					

Ordering decimals (3)

Draw a box around the largest decimal in each group.
Draw a circle around the smallest decimal in each group.

1.	0.75	0.62	0.51	0.09
2.	0.1	0.09	0.14	0.2
3.	0.95	0.8	0.76	0.08
4.	0.42	0.95	0.59	0.24
5.	1.75	0.95	1.9	1.19

Fill the missing decimals in these sequences.

1. 0.6, 0.7, 0.8, _____, 1.0

2. 0.56, 0.57, 0.58, 0.59, _____

3. 0.25, 0.30, _____, 0.40

4. 0.91, 0.93, 0.95, _____, 0.99

Order these decimal fractions and percentages from smallest to largest.

1. $\frac{1}{4}$, 0.5 , 100% , $\frac{3}{4}$

Is 75% bigger than $\frac{7}{10}$?

2. 0.2 , $\frac{1}{10}$, 75% , 0.9 , $\frac{7}{10}$, 5%

3. 15% , $\frac{1}{2}$, 0.65 , $\frac{3}{4}$, 95% , 0.25

The Fraction Book

Face, place, and total value (1)

Name:

Each number in the decimal system has a **face**, **place** and **total** value.

Face Value

The face value is always the number as it appears. For example, in the number 156…
> the number 1 has a face value of 1;
> the number 5 has a face value of 5; and
> the number 6 has a face value of 6.

Place Value

The place value is the value of the place where the number appears. For example, in the number 156…
> the number 1 has a place value of hundreds;
> the number 5 has a place value of tens; and
> the number 6 has a place value of ones.

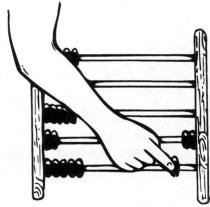

Total Value

The total value is the face value times the place value. For example, in the number 156…
> the number 1 has a total value of one hundred (100);
> the number 5 has a total value of five tens (50); and
> the number 6 has a total value of six ones (6).

Decimal fractions have the same face value but different place values to whole numbers as their value is measured in tenths, hundredths, etc. For example, in the number 1.56…
> the number 1 has a place value of 1;
> the number 5 has a place value of 5 tenths; and
> the number 6 has a place value of 6 hundredths.

Complete the place value chart for these numbers.

	Hundreds	Tens	Ones		Tenths	Hundredths
1.5				●		
7.56				●		
12.6				●		
7.98				●		
15.56				●		
243.87				●		

Face, place, and total value (2)

Name:

1. Write these decimals from their description.

    (i) A face value of 6. A place value of tenths. _____

    (ii) A face value of 9. A place value of tenths. _____

    (iii) A face value of 4. A place value of tenths. _____

    (iv) A face value of 6. A place value of hundredths. _____

    (v) A face value of 9. A place value of hundredths. _____

    (vi) The 6 has a place value of tenths.
        The 1 has a place value of hundredths. _____

    (vii) The 5 has a place value of tenths.
        The 7 has a place value of hundredths. _____

    (viii) The 1 has a place value of tens.
        The 0 has a place value of ones.
        The 7 has a place value of tenths.
        The 9 has a place value of hundredths. _____

2. Write the face, place and total value for the underlined number.

		Face Value	Place Value	Total Value
(i)	12.7̲6	_seven_	_tenths_	_0.7_
(ii)	24̲6.78	_____	_____	_____
(iii)	1.95̲	_____	_____	_____
(iv)	16̲.54	_____	_____	_____
(v)	7.0̲8	_____	_____	_____
(vi)	17.98̲	_____	_____	_____
(vii)	1.5̲6	_____	_____	_____
(viii)	7̲6.76	_____	_____	_____

Adding decimals (1)

Name:

1. Add the following decimals by coloring and then writing the answer.

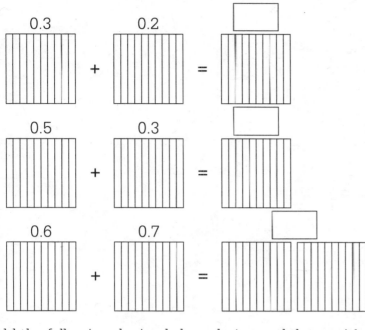

0.3 + 0.2 =

0.5 + 0.3 =

0.6 + 0.7 =

2. Add the following decimals by coloring and then writing the answer.

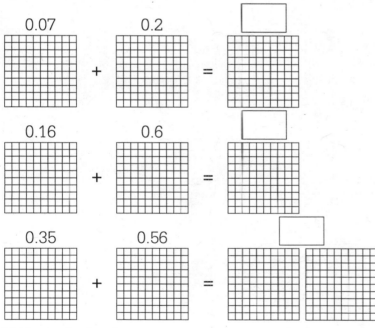

0.07 + 0.2 =

0.16 + 0.6 =

0.35 + 0.56 =

3. Add these decimals.

(i) 0.7 + 0.2 = _____

(ii) 0.2 + 0.5 = _____

(iii) 0.3 + 0.7 = _____

(iv) 0.4 + 0.8 = _____

(v) 0.13 + 0.25 = _____

(vi) 0.77 + 0.28 = _____

(vii) 0.25 + 0.75 = _____

(viii) 0.95 + 0.15 = _____

Adding decimals (2)

Name:

1. Add the following decimals by coloring and then writing the answer.

0.5   +   0.26   =   [ ]

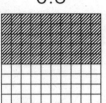 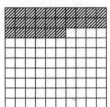 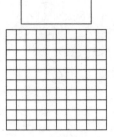

0.4   +   0.37   =   [ ]

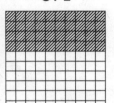 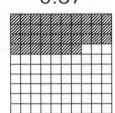 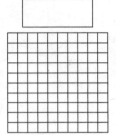

0.67   +   0.2   =   [ ]

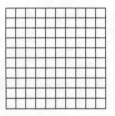 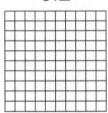 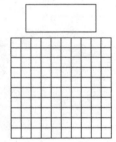

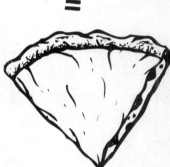

0.95   +   0.3   =   [ ]

 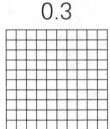 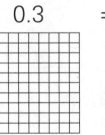 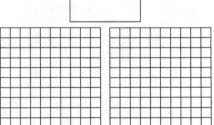

2. Add these decimals.

(i)   0.7 + 0.12 = _____

(ii)   0.12 + 0.5 = _____

(iii) 0.33 + 0.7 = _____

(iv) 0.24 + 0.18 = _____

(v)   0.13 + 0.5 = _____

(vi)   0.7 + 0.28 = _____

(vii) 0.5 + 0.75 = _____

(viii) 0.9 + 0.15 = _____

Adding decimals (3)

Name:

The simple rule when adding decimals is to always keep the decimal points in line.

For example,

$$
\begin{array}{r}
1.75 \\
+\ 0.64 \\
\hline
2.39 \\
\end{array}
$$

Complete these decimal additions.

1.
$$
\begin{array}{r}
1.7 \\
1.9 \\
+\ 2.6 \\
\hline
\\
\hline
\end{array}
$$

2.
$$
\begin{array}{r}
3.45 \\
0.72 \\
+\ 1.94 \\
\hline
\\
\hline
\end{array}
$$

3.
$$
\begin{array}{r}
1.46 \\
3.07 \\
+\ 7.94 \\
\hline
\\
\hline
\end{array}
$$

4.
$$
\begin{array}{r}
6.07 \\
1.9 \\
4.34 \\
+\ 6.8 \\
\hline
\\
\hline
\end{array}
$$

5.
$$
\begin{array}{r}
6.75 \\
7.34 \\
1.94 \\
+\ 5.65 \\
\hline
\\
\hline
\end{array}
$$

6.
$$
\begin{array}{r}
7.24 \\
5.67 \\
9.34 \\
+\ 7.89 \\
\hline
\\
\hline
\end{array}
$$

Set the following decimal additions out below and calculate the answers.

1. 1.9 + 0.7 + 6.9 + 4.2

2. 7.04 + 1.9 + 5.95 + 2.3

3. 7.64 + 9.1 + 9.43 + 5.03

4. 7.64 + 55 + 1.95 + 6.95

1.

2.

3.

4.

Subtracting decimals (1)

Name:

1. Subtract the following decimals by coloring and then writing the answer.

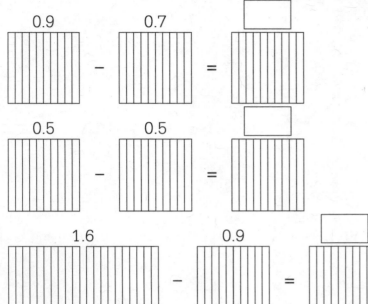

0.9   0.7   □

0.5   0.5   □

1.6   0.9   □

2. Subtract the following decimals by coloring and then writing the answer.

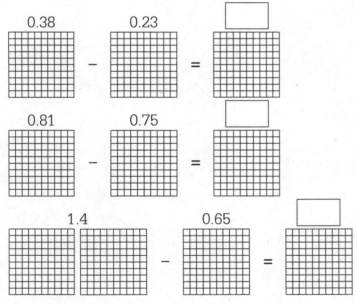

0.38   0.23   □

0.81   0.75   □

1.4   0.65   □

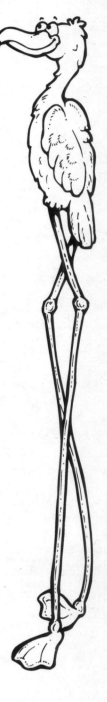

3. Subtract these decimals.

   (i) $0.52 - 0.3 = $ _____

   (ii) $0.79 - 0.28 = $ _____

   (iii) $0.75 - 0.7 = $ _____

   (iv) $0.34 - 0.18 = $ _____

   (v) $0.6 - 0.22 = $ _____

   (vi) $0.5 - 0.12 = $ _____

   (vii) $0.7 - 0.36 = $ _____

   (viii) $0.9 - 0.15 = $ _____

Subtracting decimals (2)

Name:

1. Subtract the following decimals by coloring and then writing the answer.

0.88   –   0.26   =

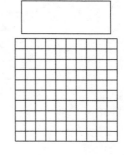 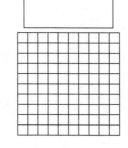  

0.4   –   0.37   =

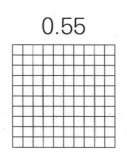 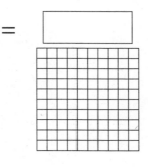 

0.70   –   0.55   =

1.28   –   0.55   =

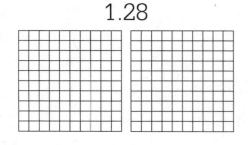 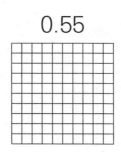 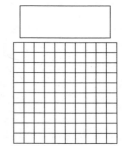

2. Subtract these decimals.

(i)   0.8   – 0.12 = _____   **(v)**   1.13 – 0.5   = _____

(ii)   0.12 – 0.05 = _____   **(vi)**   2.7   – 1.28 = _____

(iii)   0.33 – 0.1   = _____   **(vii)**   0.5   – 0.49 = _____

(iv)   0.84 – 0.18 = _____   **(viii)**   0.95 – 0.57 = _____

Subtracting decimals (3)

Name:

The rule for subtracting decimals is the same as adding. It is very important to keep the decimal point in line. For example,

$$
\begin{array}{r}
1.75 \\
-\ 0.78 \\
\hline
0.97 \\
\hline
\end{array}
$$

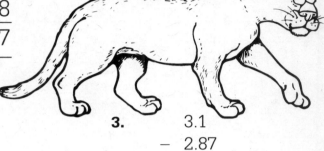

Complete these decimal subtractions.

1.
$$
\begin{array}{r}
1.9 \\
-\ 1.7 \\
\hline
\end{array}
$$

2.
$$
\begin{array}{r}
2.45 \\
-\ 0.72 \\
\hline
\end{array}
$$

3.
$$
\begin{array}{r}
3.1 \\
-\ 2.87 \\
\hline
\end{array}
$$

4.
$$
\begin{array}{r}
6.07 \\
-\ 3.9 \\
\hline
\end{array}
$$

5.
$$
\begin{array}{r}
6.55 \\
-\ 5.34 \\
\hline
\end{array}
$$

6.
$$
\begin{array}{r}
6.24 \\
-\ 5.1 \\
\hline
\end{array}
$$

7.
$$
\begin{array}{r}
3.22 \\
-\ 1.98 \\
\hline
\end{array}
$$

8.
$$
\begin{array}{r}
4.75 \\
-\ 1.34 \\
\hline
\end{array}
$$

9.
$$
\begin{array}{r}
0.94 \\
-\ 0.2 \\
\hline
\end{array}
$$

10.
$$
\begin{array}{r}
0.5 \\
-\ 0.03 \\
\hline
\end{array}
$$

11.
$$
\begin{array}{r}
11.70 \\
-\ 7.34 \\
\hline
\end{array}
$$

12.
$$
\begin{array}{r}
1.25 \\
-\ 0.25 \\
\hline
\end{array}
$$

Set the following decimal subtractions out below and calculate the answers.

1. $1.8 - 0.75$ **2.** $23 - 1.95$ **3.** $0.9 - 0.15$ **4.** $2.1 - 0.24$

1.

2.

3.

4.

Rounding to a whole number

Name:

Rounding decimal numbers occurs when a number is rounded to the decimal place or whole number that is required. For example, rounding 1.7 to the nearest whole number gives a choice of rounding up to 2 or down to 1.

Look at the number line below.

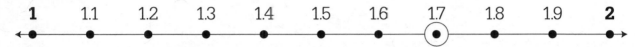

| 1 | 1.1 | 1.2 | 1.3 | 1.4 | 1.5 | 1.6 | 1.7 | 1.8 | 1.9 | 2 |

Which whole number (1 or 2) is 1.7 closest to? _____

1. Place these numbers on a number line and round to the nearest whole number.

   (i) 1.6

   | 1 | 1.1 | 1.2 | 1.3 | 1.4 | 1.5 | 1.6 | 1.7 | 1.8 | 1.9 | 2 |

   (ii) 1.3

   | 1 | 1.1 | 1.2 | 1.3 | 1.4 | 1.5 | 1.6 | 1.7 | 1.8 | 1.9 | 2 |

   (iii) 3.2

   | 3 | 3.1 | 3.2 | 3.3 | 3.4 | 3.5 | 3.6 | 3.7 | 3.8 | 3.9 | 4 |

   (iv) 2.9

   | 2 | 2.1 | 2.2 | 2.3 | 2.4 | 2.5 | 2.6 | 2.7 | 2.8 | 2.9 | 3 |

   (v) 3.6

   | 3 | 3.1 | 3.2 | 3.3 | 3.4 | 3.5 | 3.6 | 3.7 | 3.8 | 3.9 | 4 |

   (vi) 1.5

   | 1 | 1.1 | 1.2 | 1.3 | 1.4 | 1.5 | 1.6 | 1.7 | 1.8 | 1.9 | 2 |

What problems did you have with part (vi)? How did you solve these?

_____

_____

_____

2. Round these decimals to the nearest whole number.

   (i) 1.3 _____   **(ii)** 1.6 _____   **(iii)** 3.4 _____

   (iv) 2.34 _____   **(v)** 3.89 _____   **(vi)** 1.55 _____

Rounding to 1 decimal place

Name:

Rounding to one decimal place occurs when a decimal number in hundredths is rounded back to tenths.

For example, rounding 1.76 to one decimal place means that the decimal can be rounded back to 1.7 or up to 1.8. Look at the number line below.

| **1.7** | 1.71 | 1.72 | 1.73 | 1.74 | 1.75 | 1.76 | 1.77 | 1.78 | 1.79 | **1.8** |

Which is 1.76 closest to? _____

1. Place these numbers on a number line and round to one decimal place.

(i) 1.26

| **1.2** | 1.21 | 1.22 | 1.23 | 1.24 | 1.25 | 1.26 | 1.27 | 1.28 | 1.29 | **1.3** |

(ii) 1.17

| **1.1** | 1.11 | 1.12 | 1.13 | 1.14 | 1.15 | 1.16 | 1.17 | 1.18 | 1.19 | **1.2** |

(iii) 3.49

| **3.4** | 3.41 | 3.42 | 3.43 | 3.44 | 3.45 | 3.46 | 3.47 | 3.48 | 3.49 | **3.5** |

(iv) 2.93

| **2.9** | 2.91 | 2.92 | 2.93 | 2.94 | 2.95 | 2.96 | 2.97 | 2.98 | 2.99 | **3.0** |

(v) 1.03

| **1.0** | 1.01 | 1.02 | 1.03 | 1.04 | 1.05 | 1.06 | 1.07 | 1.08 | 1.09 | **1.1** |

(vi) 2.65

| **2.6** | 2.61 | 2.62 | 2.63 | 2.64 | 2.65 | 2.66 | 2.67 | 2.68 | 2.69 | **2.7** |

What problems did you have with part (vi)? How did you solve these?

_____

_____

_____

2. Round these decimals to the nearest tenth.

(i) 1.36 _____ **(ii)** 1.67 _____ **(iii)** 3.49 _____

(iv) 2.34 _____ **(v)** 3.89 _____ **(vi)** 1.55 _____

Percentages (1)

Name:

Percent, *adv.* **1.** by the hundred; for or in every hundred (used in expressing proportions, rates of interest, etc): *to get 3 percent interest.* **2.** a proportion; a percentage.

Percentage, *n.* **1.** a rate or proportion per hundred. **2.** an allowance, duty, commission, or rate of interest on a hundred. **3.** a proportion in general. **4.** *Colloq.* gain; advantage. **5. play the percentages**, to take the optimum course of action after boldly and shrewdly calculating the risks involved.

(Taken from *The Macquarie Dictionary* 1991, 2nd Edn., Macquarie Library, Sydney)

Percentages play an important part in our life. It is common to see proportions shown as percentages. For example:

In Banking

On clothing labels

In Advertising

On tests

Percentage means hundreds. Therefore 2% is $\frac{2}{100}$ or 0.02. Likewise 76% is $\frac{76}{100}$ or 0.76.

Percentages are also easy to compare. For example, in two math tests, John scored the marks shown on the right. Which of these is the better result? It is difficult to tell just by looking at these marks.

But if we express both of these marks as percentages it is easier to compare them with one another.

So John did better in the first math test.

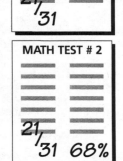

MATH TEST # 1 $\frac{14}{20}$

MATH TEST # 2 $\frac{21}{31}$

MATH TEST # 1 $\frac{14}{20}$ 70%

MATH TEST # 2 $\frac{21}{31}$ 68%

Questions

On a separate piece of paper, answer these questions about percentages.

1. In your own words describe what is meant by a percentage.

2. Is a percentage harder or easier to use than a fraction?
   Provide an example to illustrate your answer.

3. List ten uses of percentages in every day life.

4. Do you think that percentages will play a greater or lesser part in your life as you grow older? Explain your answer.

Percentages (2)

A **percentage** is a fraction of hundredths represented in another form.

For example, $\frac{20}{100}$ is a fraction. **20%** is the same number represented in a different way.

Shade these grids to show the fraction and then write the percentage.

1. $\frac{30}{100}$ = 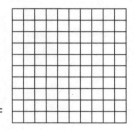 = _____ %

5. $\frac{95}{100}$ = 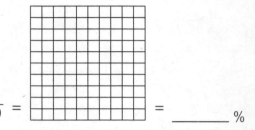 = _____ %

2. $\frac{7}{100}$ = 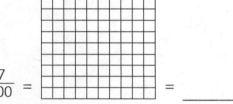 = _____ %

6. $\frac{5}{100}$ = 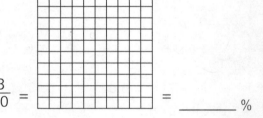 = _____ %

3. $\frac{75}{100}$ = 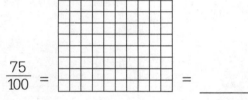 = _____ %

7. $\frac{18}{100}$ = 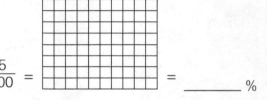 = _____ %

4. $\frac{35}{100}$ = 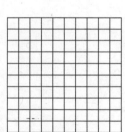 = _____ %

8. $\frac{99}{100}$ =  = _____ %

In a class mental arithmetic test these were the marks out of 100. Express them as percentages.

1. $\frac{77}{100}$ = _____ %

6. $\frac{63}{100}$ = _____ %

2. $\frac{85}{100}$ = _____ %

7. $\frac{55}{100}$ = _____ %

3. $\frac{94}{100}$ = _____ %

8. $\frac{80}{100}$ = _____ %

4. $\frac{75}{100}$ = _____ %

9. $\frac{70}{100}$ = _____ %

5. $\frac{98}{100}$ = _____ %

10. $\frac{60}{100}$ = _____ %

Fractions as percentages (1)

Name:

To convert a fraction into a percentage we must represent the fraction with a denominator of 100. To do this we follow a simple procedure. We multiply the fraction by 100 and divide the resulting numerator by the denominator. Follow the examples below:

$$\frac{1}{2} \quad x \quad \frac{100}{1} \quad = \quad \frac{100}{2} \quad = \quad \frac{50}{1} \quad = \quad 50\%$$

$$\frac{1}{4} \quad x \quad \frac{100}{1} \quad = \quad \frac{100}{4} \quad = \quad \frac{25}{1} \quad = \quad 25\%$$

$$\frac{2}{5} \quad x \quad \frac{100}{1} \quad = \quad \frac{200}{5} \quad = \quad \frac{40}{1} \quad = \quad 40\%$$

Now convert these fractions to percentages using this method.

1. $\frac{3}{4}$ x ——— = ——— = ——— = _____ %

2. $\frac{3}{5}$ x ——— = ——— = ——— = _____ %

3. $\frac{7}{10}$ x ——— = ——— = ——— = _____ %

4. $\frac{15}{20}$ x ——— = ——— = ——— = _____ %

5. $\frac{45}{50}$ x ——— = ——— = ——— = _____ %

6. $\frac{17}{25}$ x ——— = ——— = ——— = _____ %

7. $\frac{1}{4}$ x ——— = ——— = ——— = _____ %

8. $\frac{4}{5}$ x ——— = ——— = ——— = _____ %

9. $\frac{4}{10}$ x ——— = ——— = ——— = _____ %

10. $\frac{9}{10}$ x ——— = ——— = ——— = _____ %

Fractions as percentages (2)

Name:

More difficult fractions can be converted to a percentage using a calculator.

For example, $\frac{14}{31}$ can be calculated by using these steps:

1. Press ⬜1 ⬜4 to enter the numerator into the calculator.

2. Press the ⬜÷ button.

3. Press ⬜3 ⬜1 to enter the denominator.

4. Press the ⬜% button if your calculator has one. This should give an answer of 45.16%, rounded to two decimal places.

If your calculator does not have a ⬜% button, then you can do the following:

(a) Press the ⬜= button. This should give an answer of 0.45612...

(b) Press the ⬜x button, and enter ⬜1 ⬜0 ⬜0 .

(c) Press the ⬜= button, to give you the percentage, 45.16 rounded to two decimal places.

Using this method and your calculator, convert the fractions below to percentages.
Give your answer rounded off to two decimal places.

1. $\frac{4}{9}$

2. $\frac{6}{19}$

3. $\frac{4}{13}$

4. $\frac{21}{32}$

5. $\frac{23}{30}$

6. $\frac{12}{13}$

7. $\frac{13}{17}$

8. $\frac{2}{3}$

9. $\frac{7}{11}$

10. $\frac{46}{54}$

11. $\frac{18}{26}$

12. $\frac{1}{13}$

13. $\frac{3}{7}$

14. $\frac{5}{21}$

15. $\frac{7}{12}$

16. $\frac{11}{19}$

17. $\frac{44}{60}$

18. $\frac{1}{99}$

Decimals and percentages

Name:

Write the following decimals as percentages.

1. 0.6 _____
2. 0.4 _____
3. 0.56 _____
4. 0.07 _____
5. 0.25 _____

6. 0.95 _____
7. 0.01 _____
8. 0.39 _____
9. 0.7 _____
10. 0.63 _____

Write the following percentages as decimals.

1. 75% _____
2. 60% _____
3. 65% _____
4. 1% _____
5. 67% _____

6. 15% _____
7. 98% _____
8. 7% _____
9. 50% _____
10. 41% _____

The following are a student's test results as fractions. Show each grade as a %.

	Fraction	%		Fraction	%
Spelling	$\frac{19}{20}$	_____%	Mathematics	$\frac{45}{50}$	_____%
Comprehension	$\frac{8}{10}$	_____%	Health	$\frac{21}{25}$	_____%
Science	$\frac{4}{5}$	_____%	Social Studies	$\frac{7\frac{1}{2}}{10}$	_____%

The following are a student's test results expressed as a percentage.
Find the numerator for each fraction which gives this percentage.

	%	Fraction		%	Fraction
Spelling	90%	$\frac{}{10}$	Mathematics	84%	$\frac{}{25}$
Comprehension	60%	$\frac{}{5}$	Health	74%	$\frac{}{50}$
Science	75%	$\frac{}{20}$	Social Studies	75%	$\frac{}{40}$

Fractions, decimals and percentages

Name:

Write the following diagrams as fractions, decimals and percentages.

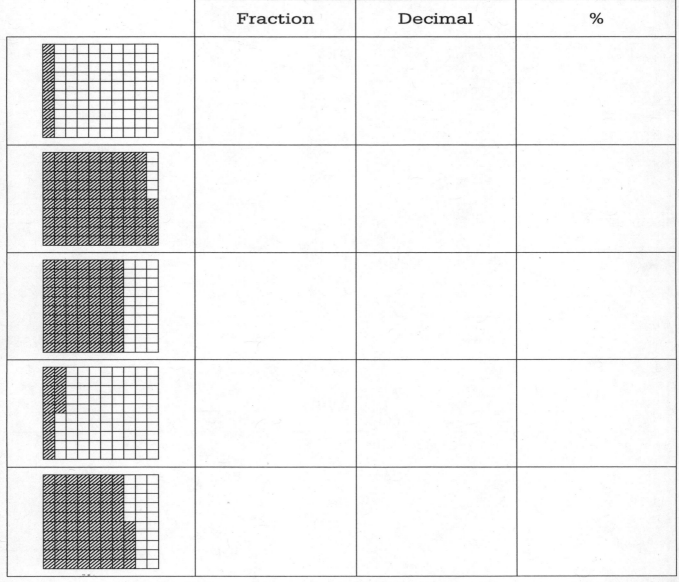

	Fraction	Decimal	%

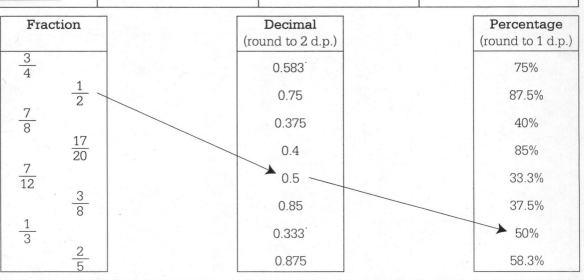

Match the fraction, decimal, and percentage.

Fraction	Decimal (round to 2 d.p.)	Percentage (round to 1 d.p.)
$\frac{3}{4}$	0.583˙	75%
$\frac{1}{2}$	0.75	87.5%
$\frac{7}{8}$	0.375	40%
$\frac{17}{20}$	0.4	85%
$\frac{7}{12}$	0.5	33.3%
$\frac{3}{8}$	0.85	37.5%
$\frac{1}{3}$	0.333˙	50%
$\frac{2}{5}$	0.875	58.3%

1. Complete these equations.

(a) $\dfrac{1}{2}$ + ⬜ = 1

(b) $\dfrac{25}{100}$ + ⬜ = 1

(c) $\dfrac{3}{10}$ + ⬜ = 1

(d) $\dfrac{2}{3}$ + ⬜ = 1

⬜ out of 4

2. Change these improper fractions to mixed numbers.

(a) $\dfrac{115}{100}$ = —— + —— = ——

(b) $\dfrac{37}{10}$ = —— + —— + —— + —— = ——

(c) $\dfrac{35}{16}$ = —— + —— + —— = ——

(d) $\dfrac{5}{3}$ = —— + —— = ——

⬜ out of 4

3. Change these mixed numbers to improper fractions.

(a) $1\dfrac{1}{4}$ = —— + —— = ——

(b) $3\dfrac{3}{4}$ = —— + —— + —— + —— = ——

(c) $2\dfrac{7}{9}$ = —— + —— + —— = ——

(d) $1\dfrac{3}{7}$ = —— + —— = ——

⬜ out of 4

4. Write two equivalent fractions for each of these fractions.

(a) $\dfrac{2}{3}$ —— ——

(b) $\dfrac{2}{5}$ —— ——

(c) $\dfrac{5}{8}$ —— ——

(d) $\dfrac{3}{4}$ —— ——

⬜ out of 4

5. Find the lowest common denominator for these fraction pairs.

(a) $\dfrac{1}{3}$, $\dfrac{1}{7}$ ⬜

(b) $\dfrac{1}{3}$, $\dfrac{1}{4}$ ⬜

(c) $\dfrac{1}{4}$, $\dfrac{1}{5}$ ⬜

(d) $\dfrac{1}{5}$, $\dfrac{1}{10}$ ⬜

⬜ out of 4

6. Find the lowest common denominator for these fraction pairs and use it to add them together.

(a) $\dfrac{1}{4}$, $\dfrac{1}{3}$ ⬜ $\dfrac{1}{4}$ + $\dfrac{1}{3}$ = —— + —— = ——

(b) $\dfrac{2}{3}$, $\dfrac{3}{4}$ ⬜ $\dfrac{2}{3}$ + $\dfrac{3}{4}$ = —— + —— = —— = ——

(c) $\dfrac{2}{5}$, $\dfrac{1}{2}$ ⬜ $\dfrac{2}{5}$ + $\dfrac{1}{2}$ = —— – —— = ——

⬜ out of 6

Review (2)

Name:

7. Express these fractions as percentages.

(a) $\frac{3}{4}$ _____ % (b) $\frac{7}{10}$ _____ %

(c) $\frac{16}{20}$ _____ % (d) $\frac{17}{25}$ _____ %

☐ out of 4

8. Use a calculator to express these fractions as percentages.

(a) $\frac{5}{9}$ _____ % (b) $\frac{7}{11}$ _____ %

(c) $\frac{21}{32}$ _____ % (d) $\frac{11}{19}$ _____ %

☐ out of 4

9. Complete this table.

Fraction	Decimal	Percentage
$\frac{1}{4}$		
	0.7	
		20%
$\frac{2}{25}$		

☐ out of 8

10. Order these groups of numbers from smallest to largest.

(a) $\frac{1}{4}$, 0.5 , 95% , $\frac{3}{4}$ _____ _____ _____ _____

(b) 0.3 , $\frac{2}{10}$, 0.95 , 75% , 5% _____ _____ _____ _____

☐ out of 2

11. Complete these decimal additions.

(a) 1.6 (b) 2.45 (c) 5.76
     1.5   0.92   1.01
  + 2.6   + 1.98   + 3.87
  _____   _____   _____

☐ out of 3

12. Complete these decimal subtractions.

(a) 1.7 (b) 8.4 (c) 0.95
  − 1.2   − 1.94   − 0.4
  _____   _____   _____

☐ out of 3

My score for this review was _____ **or** ☐ **as a decimal or** ☐ **%**

50

Parts of a whole .... page 7

1. $\dfrac{1}{2}$, $\dfrac{2}{3}$, $\dfrac{3}{5}$, $\dfrac{7}{10}$, $\dfrac{3}{4}$, $\dfrac{3}{8}$

3. $\dfrac{1}{2}$, $\dfrac{1}{3}$ $\dfrac{3}{10}$, $\dfrac{75}{100}$ $\dfrac{3}{8}$, $\dfrac{3}{4}$ $\dfrac{19}{32}$, $\dfrac{7}{10}$

Parts of a set .... page 8

1. $\dfrac{3}{4}$, $\dfrac{2}{3}$ $\dfrac{35}{100}$, $\dfrac{77}{100}$, $\dfrac{52}{100}$

3. $\dfrac{3}{10} = 0.3$, $\dfrac{6}{10} = 0.6$ $\dfrac{25}{100} = 0.25$, $\dfrac{9}{10} = 0.09$

   $\dfrac{78}{100} = 0.78$, $\dfrac{99}{100} = 0.99$

Kinds of fractions (1) .... page 9

Improper to mixed

$= \dfrac{4}{4} + \dfrac{2}{4} = 1\dfrac{2}{4}$, $= \dfrac{2}{2} + \dfrac{2}{2} + \dfrac{1}{2} = 2\dfrac{1}{2}$

Mixed to improper

$= \dfrac{6}{6} + \dfrac{5}{6} = \dfrac{11}{6}$, $= \dfrac{3}{3} + \dfrac{3}{3} + \dfrac{1}{3} = \dfrac{7}{3}$

Kinds of fractions (2) .... page 10

Improper to mixed

$1\dfrac{2}{5}$, $2\dfrac{1}{3}$, 3 $2\dfrac{7}{10}$, $1\dfrac{37}{100}$,

$2\dfrac{50}{100}$

$1\dfrac{6}{7}$, 2 , $4\dfrac{2}{5}$ $2\dfrac{4}{8}$, $1\dfrac{2}{12}$,

$2\dfrac{3}{9}$

Mixed to improper

$\dfrac{4}{3}$, $\dfrac{17}{10}$, $\dfrac{11}{4}$ $\dfrac{115}{100}$, $\dfrac{275}{100}$,

$\dfrac{13}{4}$

$\dfrac{10}{7}$, $\dfrac{33}{16}$, $\dfrac{67}{20}$ $\dfrac{87}{50}$, $\dfrac{25}{9}$, $\dfrac{5}{3}$

Equivalent fractions (1) .... page 11

1. $\dfrac{1}{2}$ $\dfrac{2}{4}$ yes

   $\dfrac{5}{10}$ $\dfrac{1}{2}$ yes

   $\dfrac{1}{5}$ $\dfrac{2}{4}$ no

2. $\dfrac{2}{4}$, $\dfrac{3}{6}$, etc.

   $\dfrac{1}{4}$, $\dfrac{4}{8}$, etc.

3. **(a)** two out of six, etc.

   (b) two out of ten, etc.

Equivalent fractions (2) .... page 12

Simplify these fractions...

1. $\dfrac{3}{4}$ (5)   2. $\dfrac{1}{5}$ (2)   3. $\dfrac{5}{6}$ (3)   4. $\dfrac{1}{2}$ (5)

Common denominator (1) .... page 13

1. 3 cars   2. 6 children
3. 7 flowers   4. 3 toys

Common denominator (2) .... page 14

1. 4   2. 10   3. 24   4. 6
5. 12   6. 10   7. 8   8. 12
9. 45   10. 36

Common denominator (3) .... page 15

1. 4   2. 10   3. 10   4. 8
5. 20

1. 21   2. 10   3. 18   4. 20
5. 100   6. 18   7. 10   8. 8

9. 12   10. 45   11. 72   12. 25

Common denominator (4) .... page 16

1. LCD = 20, $\dfrac{1}{4} + \dfrac{1}{5} = \dfrac{5}{20} + \dfrac{4}{20} = \dfrac{9}{20}$

2. LCD = 12, $\dfrac{2}{3} + \dfrac{1}{4} = \dfrac{8}{12} + \dfrac{3}{12} = \dfrac{11}{12}$

3. LCD = 10, $\dfrac{2}{5} + \dfrac{1}{2} = \dfrac{4}{10} + \dfrac{5}{10} = \dfrac{9}{10}$

4. LCD = 25, $\dfrac{17}{25} + \dfrac{1}{5} = \dfrac{17}{25} + \dfrac{5}{25} = \dfrac{22}{25}$

1. 12   2. 30   3. 20   4. 8
5. 18   6. 100

Converting to hundredths (1) .... page 17

1. 50, 0.5   2. 25, 0.25
3. 20, 0.2   4. 10, 0.1

1. 50, 0.5   5. 80, 0.8
2. 70, 0.7   6. 40, 0.4
3. 20, 0.2   7. 60, 0.6
4. 30, 0.3   8. 75, 0.75

Converting to hundredths (2) .... page 18

1. 10, 0.1   5. 30, 0.3
2. 20, 0.2   6. 4, 0.04
3. 5, 0.05   7. 68, 0.68
4. 75, 0.75   8. 80, 0.8

1. 95, $\dfrac{19}{20}$ 5. 90, $\dfrac{9}{10}$

2. 60, $\dfrac{6}{10}$ 6. 20, $\dfrac{1}{5}$

3. 75, $\dfrac{3}{4}$ 7. 2, $\dfrac{1}{50}$

4. 33, $\dfrac{1}{3}$ 8. 85, $\dfrac{17}{20}$

Ordering fractions (1) .... page 19

$\dfrac{1}{10}$, $\dfrac{1}{8}$, $\dfrac{1}{5}$, $\dfrac{1}{4}$, $\dfrac{1}{3}$, $\dfrac{1}{2}$

1. $\dfrac{10}{30}$, $\dfrac{12}{30}$, $\dfrac{15}{30}$ $\dfrac{10}{30}$, $\dfrac{12}{30}$, $\dfrac{15}{30}$

2. $\dfrac{6}{8}$, $\dfrac{4}{8}$, $\dfrac{3}{8}$ $\dfrac{3}{8}$, $\dfrac{4}{8}$, $\dfrac{6}{8}$

3. $\dfrac{30}{100}$, $\dfrac{40}{100}$, $\dfrac{15}{100}$ $\dfrac{15}{100}$, $\dfrac{30}{100}$, $\dfrac{40}{100}$

4. $\dfrac{60}{100}$, $\dfrac{70}{100}$, $\dfrac{65}{100}$ $\dfrac{60}{100}$, $\dfrac{65}{100}$, $\dfrac{70}{100}$

Ordering fractions (2) .... page 20

$\dfrac{3}{20}$, $\dfrac{3}{5}$, $\dfrac{1}{2}$, $\dfrac{3}{4}$, $\dfrac{1}{4}$, $\dfrac{1}{5}$

$\dfrac{3}{20}$, $\dfrac{1}{5}$, $\dfrac{1}{4}$, $\dfrac{1}{2}$, $\dfrac{3}{5}$, $\dfrac{3}{4}$

1. $\dfrac{3}{5}$, $\dfrac{2}{3}$, $\dfrac{7}{12}$, $\dfrac{1}{2}$ $\dfrac{1}{2}$, $\dfrac{7}{12}$, $\dfrac{3}{5}$, $\dfrac{2}{3}$

2. $\dfrac{19}{90}$, $\dfrac{4}{5}$, 1 , $\dfrac{11}{12}$ $\dfrac{19}{90}$, $\dfrac{4}{5}$, $\dfrac{11}{12}$, 1

3. $\dfrac{17}{30}$, $\dfrac{5}{8}$, $\dfrac{13}{16}$, $\dfrac{3}{10}$ $\dfrac{3}{10}$, $\dfrac{17}{30}$, $\dfrac{5}{8}$, $\dfrac{13}{16}$

4. $\dfrac{8}{15}$, $\dfrac{13}{20}$, $\dfrac{3}{4}$, $\dfrac{7}{8}$ $\dfrac{8}{15}$, $\dfrac{13}{20}$, $\dfrac{3}{4}$, $\dfrac{7}{8}$

Fractions and decimals .... page 21

1. 0.12, 0.45, 0.76, 0.34

2. (i) 0.27   (ii) 0.09   (iii) 0.75   (iv) 0.01

Centimeters and meters .... page 22

1. (i) 1.75   (ii) 1.05   (iii) 2.15   (iv) 1.76

   (v) 0.95   (vi) 3.45   (vii) 0.10   (viii) 2.71

Tenths and hundredths .... page 23

1. 0.2   2. 0.24   3. 0.9   4. 0.65
5. 0.07   6. 0.5   7. 1.47   8. 2.01
9. 0.70   10. 0.80

Ordering decimals (1) .... page 24

1. 0.6, 0.8, 0.2, 0.9
   In order: 0.2, 0.6, 0.8, 0.9
2. 0.99, 0.06, 0.54, 0.45
   In order: 0.06, 0.45, 0.54, 0.99
3. 0.09, 0.1, 0.11, 0.21, 0.8
4. 0.09, 0.11, 0.27, 0.55, 0.61
5. 0.4 is ten times bigger than 0.04.

Ordering decimals (2) .... page 25

1. 0.8, 0.5, 0.2, 0.3
   In order: 0.2, 0.3, 0.5, 0.8
2. 0.23, 0.32, 0.87, 0.78
   In order: 0.23, 0.32, 0.78, 0.87
3. (i) 0.3   (ii) 0.32   (iii) 0.5   (iv) 0.87
4. one tenth
5. 0.04, 0.3, 0.34, 0.4, 0.43, 0.56, 0.57, 0.75

Ordering decimals (3) .... page 26

1. largest = 0.75   smallest = 0.09
2. largest = 0.2   smallest = 0.09
3. largest = 0.95   smallest = 0.08
4. largest = 0.95   smallest = 0.24
5. largest = 1.9   smallest = 0.95

Ordering decimals (3) (cont.)...........page 26

1. 0.9   **2.** 0.60   **3.** 0.35   **4.** 0.97

1. $\dfrac{1}{4}$, 0.5 , $\dfrac{3}{4}$, 100%

2. 5% , $\dfrac{1}{10}$, 0.2 , $\dfrac{7}{10}$, 75% , 0.9

3. 15% , 0.25 , $\dfrac{1}{2}$, 0.65 , $\dfrac{3}{4}$, 95%

Face, place and total value (1) .... page 27

hundreds	tens	ones		tenths	hundredths
0	0	1	•	5	0
0	0	7	•	5	6
0	1	2	•	6	0
0	0	7	•	9	8
0	1	5	•	5	6
2	4	3	•	8	7

Face, place and total value (2) .... page 28

1. **(i)** 0.6   **(ii)** 0.9   **(iii)** 0.4   **(iv)** 0.06
   (v) 0.09   **(vi)** 0.61   **(vii)** 0.57   **(viii)** 10.79

2. **(ii)** four   tens   40
   (iii) five   hundredths   0.05
   (iv) six   ones   6
   (v) zero   tenths   0
   (vi) eight   hundredths   0.08
   (vii) five   tenths   0.5
   (viii) seven   tens   70

Adding decimals (1) .... page 29

1. 0.5, 0.8, 1.3
2. 0.27, 0.76, 0.91
3. **(i)** 0.9   **(ii)** 0.7   **(iii)** 1.0   **(iv)** 1.2
   (v) 0.38   **(vi)** 1.05   **(vii)** 1   **(viii)** 1.1

Adding decimals (2) .... page 30

1. 0.76, 0.77, 0.87, 1.25
2. **(i)** 0.82   **(ii)** 0.62   **(iii)** 1.03   **(iv)** 0.42
   (v) 0.63   **(vi)** 0.98   **(vii)** 1.25   **(viii)** 1.05

Adding decimals (3) .... page 31

1. 6.2   **2.** 6.11   **3.** 12.47   **4.** 19.11
5. 21.68   **6.** 30.14

1. 13.7   **2.** 17.19   **3.** 31.2   **4.** 71.54

Subtracting decimals (1) .... page 32

1. 0.2, 0, 0.7
2. 0.15, 0.06, 0.75
3. **(i)** 0.22   **(ii)** 0.51   **(iii)** 0.05   **(iv)** 0.16
   (v) 0.38   **(vi)** 0.38   **(vii)** 0.34   **(viii)** 0.75

Subtracting decimals (2) .... page 33

1. 0.62, 0.03, 0.15, 0.73
2. **(i)** 0.68   **(ii)** 0.07   **(iii)** 0.23   **(iv)** 0.66
   (v) 0.63   **(vi)** 1.42   **(vii)** 0.01   **(viii)** 0.38

Subtracting decimals (3) .... page 34

1. 0.2   **2.** 1.73   **3.** 0.23   **4.** 2.17
5. 1.21   **6.** 1.14   **7.** 1.24   **8.** 3.41

9. 0.74   **10.** 0.47   **11.** 4.36   **12.** 1

1. 1.05   **2.** 21.05   **3.** 0.75   **4.** 1.86

Rounding to a whole number .... page 35

1. **(i)** 2   **(ii)** 1   **(iii)** 3   **(iv)** 3
   (v) 4   **(vi)** 2
2. **(i)** 1   **(ii)** 2   **(iii)** 3   **(iv)** 2
   (v) 4   **(vi)** 2

Rounding to 1 decimal place .... page 36

1. **(i)** 1.3   **(ii)** 1.2   **(iii)** 3.5   **(iv)** 2.9
   (v) 1.0   **(vi)** 2.6
2. **(i)** 1.4   **(ii)** 1.7   **(iii)** 3.5   **(iv)** 2.3

   (v) 3.9   **(vi)** 1.6

Percentages (1) No answers .... page 37

Percentages (2) .... page 38

1. 30%   **2.** 7%   **3.** 75%   **4.** 35%
5. 95%   **6.** 5%   **7.** 18%   **8.** 99%

1. 77%   **2.** 85%   **3.** 94%   **4.** 75%
5. 98%   **6.** 63%   **7.** 55%   **8.** 80%
9. 70%   **10.** 60%

Fractions as percentages (1) .... page 39

1. 75%   **2.** 60%   **3.** 70%   **4.** 75%
5. 90%   **6.** 68%   **7.** 25%   **8.** 80%
9. 40%   **10.** 90%

Fractions as percentages (2) .... page 40

1. 44.44%   **2.** 31.58%   **3.** 30.77%
4. 65.62%   **5.** 76.67%   **6.** 92.31%
7. 76.47%   **8.** 66.67%   **9.** 63.64%
10. 85.19%   **11.** 69.23%   **12.** 7.69%
13. 42.86%   **14.** 23.81%   **15.** 58.33%
16. 57.89%   **17.** 73.33%   **18.** 1.01%

Decimals and percentages .... page 41

Spelling = 95%   Mathematics = 90%
Comprehension = 80%   Health = 84%
Science = 80%   Social Studies = 75%

Spelling = $\dfrac{9}{10}$ Mathematics = $\dfrac{21}{25}$

Comprehension = $\dfrac{3}{5}$ Health = $\dfrac{37}{50}$

Science = $\dfrac{15}{20}$ Social Studies = $\dfrac{30}{40}$

Fractions, decimals and percentages .... page 42

$\dfrac{10}{100} = 0.1 = 10\%$

$\dfrac{95}{100} = 0.95 = 95\%$

$\dfrac{70}{100} = 0.7 = 70\%$

$\dfrac{15}{100} = 0.15 = 15\%$

$\dfrac{75}{100} = 0.75 = 75\%$

$\dfrac{3}{4} = 0.75 = 75\%$ $\dfrac{1}{2} = 0.5 = 50\%$

$\dfrac{7}{8} = 0.875 = 87.5\%$ $\dfrac{17}{20} = 0.85 = 85\%$

$\dfrac{7}{12} = 0.583 = 58.3\%$ $\dfrac{3}{8} = 0.375 = 37.5\%$

$\dfrac{1}{3} = 0.333 = 33.3\%$ $\dfrac{2}{5} = 0.4 = 40\%$

Review (1) .... page 43

1. (a) $\dfrac{1}{2}$ (b) $\dfrac{75}{100}$
(c) $\dfrac{7}{10}$ (d) $\dfrac{1}{3}$

2. (a) $1\dfrac{15}{100}$ (b) $3\dfrac{7}{10}$
(c) $2\dfrac{3}{16}$ (d) $1\dfrac{2}{3}$

3. (a) $\dfrac{5}{4}$ (b) $\dfrac{15}{4}$
(c) $\dfrac{25}{9}$ (d) $\dfrac{10}{7}$

5. (a) 21   (b) 12
(c) 20   (d) 10

6. (a) $12, = \dfrac{3}{12} + \dfrac{4}{12} = \dfrac{7}{12}$
(b) $12, = \dfrac{8}{12} + \dfrac{9}{12} = \dfrac{17}{12} = 1\dfrac{5}{12}$
(c) $10, = \dfrac{4}{10} + \dfrac{5}{10} = \dfrac{9}{10}$

Review (2) .... page 44

7. (a) 75%   (b) 70%
(c) 80%   (d) 68%

8. (a) 55.6%   (b) 63.6%
(c) 65.6%   (d) 57.9%

9. $\dfrac{1}{4}$ 0.25   25%
$\dfrac{7}{10}$ 0.7   70%
$\dfrac{1}{5}$ 0.2   20%
$\dfrac{2}{25}$ 0.08   8%

10. (a) $\dfrac{1}{4}$, 0.5, $\dfrac{3}{4}$, 95%

(b) 5%, $\dfrac{2}{10}$, 0.3, 75%, 0.95

11. (a) 5.7   (b) 5.35   (c) 10.64

12. (a) 0.5   (b) 6.46   (c) 0.55